Born in Manchester, Stephen Belowsky honed his craft writing poetry in New York's Lower East Side through the 1980s.

He later became immersed in the anti-folk scene at the Sidewalk Café and the Bowery Poetry Club, where his work developed a steady following.

Writing on San Francisco, LA and the East Coast, he gained equal inspiration from Hollywood, whilst performing at The Standard hotel on Sunset Boulevard.

His poems are marked by a journalistic urgency, appearing in various magazines as well as recordings on Alan McGee's Creation23 label. This is his first collected volume of poetry.

"Stephen Belowsky runs with words... the words tumble out and run away with him in mad capricious gallops. Possibly because dyslexia jumbles up the word-world in him, Belowsky obsessively fumbles with them forcing a coherence and odd juxtapositions that would not occur to the rest of us.
His poetry is a self-medicating lexicon of understanding that is unique and exhilarating… "

– Sir Bob Geldof

"Somewhere there is a planet full of words, and Belowsky's got first dibs on it. There, he hones each one into the pinnacle of the art of the spoken word. Fortunately, his incisive, witty and tender observations sound just as good on the page.
A Poet Laureate for LA, New York, Manchester!"

– Sam Burcher
The International Times

"He's always surprising — you think you know where the poem is going, then he throws a line that catches you off guard."

– Simon Astaire

"There is absolutely no one — poet or otherwise — like him on Planet Earth."

– Sebastian de Souza

HONK

HONK

Stephen Belowsky

020-DESK-ZERO

020-DESK-ZERO
Publishing imprint and
24-hour telephone line.

First UK Edition, 2026
ISBN 978-1-9195196-1-6

 A CIP record for this book is available from the British Library.

With thanks to Milo Astaire, Finn Constantine, Christie Sistrunk (for her extensive editorial support), the Estate of Ken Price, Colin Donnelly, and Matthew Marks Gallery.

Printed and bound in
Great Britain by TJ Books
Distributed in the UK by
Public Knowledge Books
Edited by Christie Sistrunk
Design by James Jessiman

HONK

Poems 1987 — 2026

F O R E W O R D

Renegade wordsmith and master of machine gun prose, Stephen Belowsky is the maverick's maverick – a poet whose words are stripped down to their powerful core.

Just like all the greatest rock and roll from AC/DC to the Stooges and punk rock, it was about the power of minimalism.

Stephen Belowsky (or more minimally '*Belowsky*'), demonstrates how the real art was saying everything with as little as possible – the art of making the perfect statement with a poetic instinct.

Honk collects poetry by the underground Mancunian legend and nomadic citizen of the fierce free world, now residing in Perth, Australia.

Here Belowsky shows he understands the power of the word and inhabits its sharp prose, making a meaning out of the chaos with his pop culture missives and startling imagery.

—John Robb

REASONS FOR ENTERING THE U.S.

Double double cheese
Fries and a shake
A loose joint between my lips
So I can get high upon the sunset strip

THE BEST DAMN SLICE

I've found the
Best damn slice
Of pizza down in
New York Town
Don't want you around

Well, the Donald may have
His millions and zillions
And the beggar man's
Got his dimes
But they both share
The common ground
Because what they don't know
Is CNN Breaking News…

Yo! Belowsky says:

"Hey - I've found
The best damn slice
Of pizza down in
New York Town
Don't want the Zagat Review
Coming around
Followed by the Daily News
Followed by Sarah J. Parker
Followed by her adoring Matthew
Carrying his Tony paperweight
Followed by Paris
Followed by the Knicks
Followed by the Kabbalah
Followed by Scientology
Followed by Jews for Jesus

Followed by Bloomberg
Followed by Hillary
Followed by Bubba
Followed by 50 Cent
Followed by a blaze
A blaze
A blaze
Of bullets
Followed by second-rate
Second-rate Jersey Rockers
Followed by Howard the Shock Jock
Followed by late-night lap dancers
Followed by pseudo-gangsters
Stay away paparazzi
'Coz this is my pizza place"

Some may say:

"I know the best damn slice
In this Manhattan place"

Well
I scorn
I scorn
I scorn
In your ignorant
Pepperoni face

I've heard them say:

"Yo! Belowsky
Is it on Bleecker
Is it on Spring
Or down on Houston

Is it Famous Ray's
Or Famous Ben's
Or Famous Joes's?"

"No
No
No
It ain't none of those"

Heard them say:

"Yo! Belowsky
Is it in the water
Is it in the dough
It's in the Gotham air?"
I've heard these alley cats
Talking the same old crap
Well I challenge that

I heard them say:

"Yo, Belowsky
Is it the East Side
Is it the West Side
Is it Uptown
Is it Midtown
Is it Downtown
Is it on Second
Is it on Third
Or, as Bob Dylan says
Positively Fourth?"
Well, I have it
Written down
In cryptic code

Sitting in a Morgan Stanley
Safe deposit box
You see not even Chase
Not even Chase
Not even Chase
Can have a taste

This pizza place
Seems so empty
Seems to close so early
The phones are disconnected
No deliveries are expected
And you may ask the yellow cab
To cruise around

Say:
"Yo, Mohammed
Take me to the best damn
Slice of pizza down in
New York Town"
But in garlic I trust
That the crust is too thick
The crust is too thin
And the cab meter
Is a-ticking
And for me to tell you
This magic location
You know what you're
Gonna have to do?
You're gonna have to
Gun me down

See I'll happily die
I'll happily die

I'll happily die
In a slimy messy
Tomato base
You can lay me to rest
In a giant pizza box
And stick a massive
Olive on top

Maybe this is just some kind of
Figment of my imagination
Some kind of crazy
Mozzarella creation
And welcome to my mind
Because in that mind is
The best damn slice of pizza
Down in New York Town
Period

For Andrew Hoepfner
He knows the pizza place

For James Jessiman… you're still searching...
head towards 14th Street then West

I RUN WITH WORDS

I run with words
That are all
Jumbled up
'Till they make
Situations
Creations
Of misquotations
Of my spell-checked
Dyslexic imagination

I run with words
To the oddest of places
No intellectual literature
Can take me
Supermarket checkouts
Mystical temples
Netflix
Downloaded
Rentals

I find myself
Writing as I'm
Walking
And talking
To art galleries
And stages
Find cryptic words
To stay with
Rearrange with
Help to trace
Races
Political rages

Anti-gun law
Crazies

Cryptic words
That are
Crass
And tasteless
That can become
Politically dangerous
Like a mad fire
Raging
That needs relocating

See
The world needs
Something more
Soothing
Soothing
And melodical

But must return
Comical
Formatted to fit
My dyslexic
In simple form
Majestic
Word-sharp
Almost electric
Written by a mad poet
Eccentric
That leads you
Down paragraphs
Of twisted
Deception

You find yourself
In the new written
Religion
Of cosmic
Conclusion

May change
Your dreams
In rhyme
In time
That gets you
On a lyrical
Celebrity payroll
A laureate misfit
In some neon-modified
Online university
Some kind of
Sublime
Obscurity
These are
Cryptic words
To play with
Sell to the
Highest bidder
Or dismantled
Stolen
And put on
Twitter
Or a new format
That you're trying
To figure

You're a
Demented
Ziggy Stardust
Ziggy Stardust
Ziggy Stardust
New generation
Writer

Words
Spread across
The universe
Hitting satellites
Outside atmospheres
Spell-checked
And translated into
One thousand translations
That hits every
Lost civilization

But it all
Starts with
A word
Or
A verb
For a
New world
That always
Turns in
One direction

And I run with words
That are all
Jumbled up
'Till they make

Situations
Creations
Of misquotations
Of my
Spell-checked
Dyslexic
Imagination

I run with words
To the oddest of places
No intellectual literature
Can take me
Supermarket checkouts
Mystical temples
Netflix
Downloaded
Rentals

For Christie
You heard it first

CONS

In my cons
I am
Immovable
Radical
Antisocial
Dysfunctional
Confrontational
And fucking dangerous

In my Converse cons
I am always
Moving
Grooving
Dirt-talking
Punching
Walking onstage
Around trouble
Writing poetic stance
Aggravating the mind
No censorship
No sales pitch
Yet I will take
The dollars
And split

In my cons
I never compromise
Never waiting
Always creating
Running and escaping
Always relocating

In my cons
My mind is controlled
By my worn-out soles
'Till my toes come through
Stinking at you

In my cons
I'm always blue
Always ready to
Look you in the eye
And negotiate with you

In my cons
I may sound like some
TV sneaker commercial
But this ain't no rehearsal
No sweet residual.

In my cons
I will turn up the amp
Check you out
'Till I see
A blue flashing light
In the rear view
Depress the clutch
4 on the floor
I will fight for you
Never desert the cause
In my cons
I will occupy
Philosophize
Capitalize

In my cons
I will never lie
Yet in my cons
I will watch you die

If it's right
It's wrong
And if it's wrong
It's right

In my cons
My mind is free
I see no religion
See no colour
See no white collar
See no gangster

In my cons
I'm always
Standing
Standing
Standing
Standing in
The fading light

For Patti, I was always heading out to NJ, straight out of Penn, always in my cons. Meet me at the diner.

76 GAS

76 Gas is cool
Big orange ball
Sits high in the sky
Hypnotic orange ball
Is calling you

Don't get gas
No place except
The big orange ball
In the sky

76 Americana
76 I don't know
Some place
Out in the gulf

But on Wilshire I see
The big orange ball
In the sky and
It's home to me

Cool orange ball
Addictive orange ball
Cool in the sky
24 hours a day
It's just an orange ball day

And I can see those
Jet fighters somewhere
Out in the gulf
But on Wilshire I see
The big orange ball

In the sky and
It's home to me

Cool orange ball
Cool in the sky
24 hours a day
It's just an
Orange ball day

MALL OF AMERICA

1990s park the car
In a 10-storey car park
You and me were
Forever groovy in
A man-made place
Called Camp Snoopy
Hitting the ATM
Taking twenties
And giving it back again
Walking through
The malls of America

Walking through
Nature's Cove
Benetton and the Gap
You and me forever groovy
In a man-made place
Called Camp Snoopy
You and me interactive
Consumers in love
With an Estée Lauder smile
And Estée Lauder lips
She looked so
Post-modern romantic

With Victoria's Secret
She looked so sexy
With a hat by Ralph Lauren
She looked so comical
With a haircut by Vidal Sassoon
She looked so unusual
With lenses in less than an hour

She looked so 20-20

With bags of Godiva chocolates
She looked so fucking greedy
With a classic novel from
Barnes & Noble she looked
So intellectual

As a promotions girl sprayed her
With a new formulated
Calvin Klein scent she was
So unapproachable

With Visa
With Master
She was so
Irrational

As we entered a
17- screen AMC
To take in a romantic
Julia Robert's rom-com movie
She became so popcorn
And Coke emotional
In the 10-storey
Giant
Ugly
Concrete
Car park
We felt so lost

As I awoke from a dream
And I realized all the
Franchises found us so

Usable
Like a Gillette Blue 2 blade
So disposable
As I tried a return
On a shirt I found
There's no refunds
No exchanges
All sales are final
It's a Corporate Bible
And as we left that car park
And looked back
In total amazement
I turned to my lady and said:

"Hey give us another
See's Candy
Let's go home
Put on a Music Land DVD
Of the sold-out Kenny G"
And as we left that car park
And looked back
In total amazement
I realized we were just
Another mesmerized couple
And I realized it was just
Another fucking mall
Lost
Lost
Lost
Lost in the middle
of America

For Karen
For Minneapolis
Thank you

RACE TO SAVE THE 21ST CENTURY

Racing now
And the first
To show
On the inside
Utopia

Out of Godly Intervention
Mystical Ideas and
Human Ideology
Got off to an absolute flier
As too did Advancement
And Technology out of
Seattle Washington
Sponsored by Starbucks Coffee
Caffeine constantly
Percolating through the veins
Owned and trained by Mr. Bill Gates
Running on nicely

They're being closely followed
By Global Warming
Out of the Greenhouse Effect
And Total Human Destruction
Of the Rainforest
Heating it up now
And sweating it out
Through the middle
Then comes Third World Debt
Being heavily hampered
By the Fluctuating Dollar
The Volatile Euro
And a New World Order

And as they start to
Settle down now
They're being pressed
By World Hunger
Out of Africa and
The Southern Hemisphere
Looking terribly
Terribly skinny
On the rails
And with absolutely
Nowhere to go

Three back
Two wide now
Is A Deadly Virus
Not much known about
This little puppy but looking
Looking pretty impressive
Under the microscope

And tailing off the field now
Thermonuclear War
Out of the hydrogen
And the atom
Seemed to have
Dropped out of it
Towards the end
Of the 20th century
Buts fallen into some
Dangerous–radical–hands
Of late and seems to be
Hanging in there
As they come into the dip

Advancement and Technology
Has broken down
And dropped out of it
Altogether
So too has World Hunger
And Third World Debt
But Global Warming's
Taking up the challenge now!

It's Global Warming
Two lengths from
A Deadly Virus, who says:

"Wait a minute, Charlie
It's not over yet"

As they come into the turn
Global Warming starts to tire
As A Deadly Virus
Gets up on the inside
It's A Deadly Virus
From Global Warming
But wait a minute...
Here comes Thermonuclear War
Down the grandstand side now!
It's Thermonuclear War
Getting up on
A Deadly Virus

And at the line that's the way
The 21st century ends
Thermonuclear War
A Deadly Virus
Global Warming

Third World Debt
World Hunger
And way
Way
Way back
In the field
Nowhere
To be
Seen…

Utopia

THE QUAKER MAN

Quaker Man smiles
On the morning box of oats
He's got a double chin
And big red cheeks
And he never lets you down
He just smiles

And she can give you
The worst night of your life
But the Quaker Man will
Be there top shelf smiling
Saying:

"Hey you down there
Don't you worry about
That miserable bitch
Up in the bedroom
Ho-ho-ho I am the
Quaker Man"

And then you go
To wherever
You think thank God
For the Quaker Man

You think
Thank God for the oats

MIDTOWN

Moving through Midtown
Riding a yellow cab
Past a stressed-out NY City
All the networks are
Draining my creativity
Want to say to the cab driver:

"Yo Mohammed
Kennedy
Get on-board a Richard Branson
Virgin Atlantic Flight Fantastic
Back to a red passport
Pan-European identity"

But you're locked
In negotiations
Using imagination
An actor friend from
the West Side says:

"Confide in me"

I say:

"You must be crazy
Playing your surreal roles
Living off pizza slices
Diet Coke
Captain Crunch
KitKat
And Xanax
Driving your nervous system

Fucking crazy
You're just as insane as me"

Moving the Bic pen
Across a napkin
Sinking the caffeine
And running the
Jackie 'O' Reservoir daily
Running the
Jackie 'O' Reservoir
Like Dustin Hoffman's
Marathon Man

Around
And around
And around
The park you go
At a neurotic pace
And you're wired
To your iPhone
And you're wired
To Mozart
And to make it funny
And to make it dramatic
And to make it great
And to make it sell
It's going to take
A lot of medical help
From a Park Avenue
Analyst's couch
To a 24-hour
Duane Reade's
Pharmaceutical shelf

As I step out
Onto 73rd and 3rd
The cab meter reads
Under $10
Wow you think
It's another
Manhattan miracle
And another day for a writer
To take on the dreams
Of liberty
Of the illegal immigrants
Of the workers
The doctors
The lawyers
The dentists filling cavities
The pan handlers
The begger men
And the thieves
And you want to call
Your girl in a hurry
Excited
1-800-collect
And say:

"Wow, what an
Incredible - fantastic
Unbelievable mess"

As you're moving
Through Midtown
Riding a yellow cab
Past a stressed-out NY City
Just want to say to the cab driver:

"Yo Mohammed
Yo Mohammed
Yo Mohammed
Take me back
Take me back
Take me back
To Kennedy"

For Melanie Einzig
The finest street photographer in NYC

BETWEEN THE LINES

Like every poet
That ever followed
The shadow of
Mr. Bob Dylan
One song is sung
A-brainstorming
A-thousand ways
And they come back again
To see it change
Again and again

And they descend on
Stadiums and lawns
In streets
Universities
Penitentiaries
From Wall Street
To the Village
To Spanish Harlem
Carrying a six-string
Like a submachine gun
Firing words
And metaphors
Ideas
Spoken words

Speaking to
Generations
Reflections
Ripples on the oceans
Railroads
Driving roads

Comedic lines
Hidden behind
Love and politics
Religion and fate

Mystic
Magical
Whimsical
Converse
Conversation
Childish and pure

Look north
Look south
Look east
Look west
There's candlelight
Flickering on the horizon
That will never flicker out.
It's always gonna be
Blowing in the wind
And on the freezing plains
Of Duluth Minnesota
To Dinkytown
A lone stiletto disappears
In the snowstorm
Born Robert Zimmerman

Dances between the lines
But infinite
That will travel
Beyond our galaxies
It will travel beyond time
Burning bright

Forever young
Forever young
Forever young
Forever as
Mr. Bob Dylan

HONK

Honk
In the early 90's
We drove around in cars
Our emotional warehouses
Hung on off-ramps
Honking our horns
For a man in a vegetable hat
Saying "Ban the bomb"
And if the crowd outside
The Federal Building
Shouted "Honk!"
We'd damn well honk
Yeah we'd honk for anything

War
Peace
The IRA
CIA
Communism
Zionism
A man called Mandela
In the Southern hemisphere
Coca Cola
Coca Cola Classic
Save the local school hall
An undertaker who lost
The President's body
On the way to a funeral
Abortion
Anti-abortion
Save the Whales
The females

The Evergreens
The Hollywood sign

Yeah we'd honk
Til the batteries
In the car went dead
And there was
No more honk
Left in us

I AM ME, I AM YOU

Bring in the jets
Bring in the MiGs
Come on Castro
Come on Kennedy
Come swim with Che
In the Bay of Pigs

Ideology is simple, man
It's food and drink
For everyone
I'm Argentinian
Mexican
Bolivian
Guatemalan
Cuban
Uruguayan
Just South American

Ask the CIA
As they walk my way
I'm no revolutionary
Just fighting poverty
Fight
Fight
Fight
For human rights
A guerilla in the mist
Ideology is simple, man
It's food and drink
For everyone
I can give you times
A motorcycling

Medical student
With diaries on the road
A fly-half rugby union man
No inequalities
No alienation
Just rebellion
Ideology is simple, man
It's food and drink
For everyone

Trapped like a bloody pig
Two bullets in the legs
Surrounded by 1,800
In the Vela Grande mud
Tied up ready for
The executioner
He looked into the eyes
Of Mario Terán and said:

"Shoot me
And shoot yourself
I am me
I am you
I am every man
Before you shoot
just a few last words
Ideology is simple, man
It's food and drink
For everyone"

DUMP THE STOCK

1980s
It flowed like Niagara Falls
Money out the wall
Food made of noodles
CDs that sparkled
Reincarnation
Blue jeans from the Gap
Bought on paper greens
Out the wall
It flowed
It flowed
It flowed
Like Niagara Falls

Benetton raced by
A European racetrack
Sat down on 5th Avenue
Everybody laughed
And laughed
'Till a Monday in October
When a voice cried out
From the floor:

"Dump the stock
Oh, baby baby
Dump the fucking lot"
And my brother cried
As he gave a MG back
And sat with the cat
Then said with a smile:
"I'll be back on
A Benetton racetrack"

Then we all walked
Down 5th Avenue
We all walked onto
Wall street
And we all sat down
And had ice-whipped
Coffee mochas
We paid in quarters
Because no greens
Would come out the wall
On the Avenue
No more
No more
No more
But for one second
There back in the 1980s
It flowed green
It flowed
It flowed
It flowed
like Niagara Falls
'Till a Monday in October
When a voice cried out
from the floor:

"Sell - sell - sell!"
When a voice cried out:

"Dump the stock
Oh, baby baby
Dump the fucking lot!"*

For LT —
You always had one eye on the coffee and bagel, one eye on The Dow

5TH AVENUE TRASH

Looky here
Across the street
You ever see
Your trash so neat?
It ain't a drag
It's in the bag
Got to be a whole lot better
Than under your feet

Now this old couple
Must have been blind
They threw their dollar bills
Down the chute
And guess who found them?
It was the Donald standing in his suit

And looky here
Across the street
You ever see
Your trash so neat?
It ain't a drag
It's in the bag
Got to be a whole lot better
Than under your feet
Right on!

DUNKIN' DONUTS

Dunkin' into Dunkin' Donuts
I take the week's first coffee sup
Pick up a GQ mag
A six pack of abs
Stares back at me
As I bite down on
My Monday morning
Boston Cream
I want to scream

GQ take me away to
A land of airbrushed reality
Spray away
Start with my personality
Airbrush my lies and the
American Psycho consumer eyes
Put me in some kind of GQ disguise
Throw me in a pit
And well give me
The Brad bits

And airbrush me some
Fab credit
A Chase card
With loads of debit
Airbrush me from a
Dirty old Corolla
To a shiny new Roller
A John Travolta dance move
His 707 plane and his
Scientology game
And airbrush me

A massive Dirk Diggler
The biggest in the world
And throw in a Roller Girl
To give it a twirl

And airbrush me
To centre court
Where I crash an ace
Down the line
Then get down
And kiss the ground
As I pick up the Wimbledon crown
Have a championship dance
With Venus Williams
And say to the British press
"It's all black and white
And baby that's all right!"

And I tell the world
Of my mega peace plan
That will save the rainforests
And mankind as I bite down
One more time on
My Second Avenue Dunkin' Donut
Monday morning Boston Cream
I want to fucking scream

COCO

With a tear somewhere
A stitch in time
A needle
Chalk
Paris
Rain
Spring
Summer
Winter
A war
A truce
A life

The start of the A-list
Velvet rope
Perfume
Writers
Actors
Composers
Coco
Coco
Avant-Chanel

A stitch
A hem
A thread
Simple lines
Black and white
White and black
Perfection
Coco
Coco

Coco
Number 5
Coco
Coco
Avant-Chanel

GURU NUMBER ONE

43 — 21
The life of a working-class guru
Has only just begun
Not easy to become a guru
How many hours does a guru work?

I'll tell you
5 guru hours
Equals a 40-hour week
But does a guru get 8 hours sleep?
And what wheat does a guru eat?

So go find yourself a guru
'Coz it's not cryptic code
'Coz hey, now you can
Google your guru
Or go straight to
www.guru.com
Or wait for that guru
To materialize
Don't be surprised
Because a guru could
Always come in disguise

Yo! There he goes
Down Fifth Avenue
Check that smile
That ain't no average smile
That's the smile of a
Real-living-loving guru
Free and on the loose
A London guru

A New York guru
An LA guru
A P.R. guru
An Ad guru
A media guru
A finance guru
A guru at the Château

'Coz a guru's not restricted
No more to no Himalayan cave
The guru's broken free from
All those weird-freaky-sheets
It's Armarni suits with a perfect
Guru fit
Prada shoes
And Bulgari jewels

No Lama guru
No Ghandi guru
No Maharishi guru
No Hendrix guru
No Marley guru
No Lennon guru
Definitely no dead gurus
Only living-loving gurus

And no longer do gurus
Tell time from the sun
It's a Rolex man
And every guru has one
And the car number plate's
Simple up on Sunset Boulevard
It's Guru Number One

And at the airport you've got
Club Lounge
Exec Lounge
And you guessed it…
You got the Guru Lounge
A place where all the gurus
Connect and subscribe to
Guru Weekly
Some fly first
Some fly second
I fly the only way I know
And that's Guru Class

And catch him tonight on CNN
As Anderson Cooper investigates
The sweet life of the guru
And asks the question:

"Is there a hidden guru
Lying dormant
Dormant
Dormant
Dormant
Within you?
Is there a guru
Ready to jump out
Speculate
Negotiate
And communicate?"

Tonight all will be answered
As Anderson investigates
In a two-hour special

Not to be missed
You – Me – and the Mysteries
Of the Contemporary Guru
Now available on YouTube

So go find that magic tag
Tag goo
Tag goo goo
Tag goo goo goo
Tag goo
Tag all of you

For Simon Astaire
The original Guru Number One

HOOKS JABS & WORDS

Black
White
Yellow
All the skin in my world
Bleeds red
When fighters step through
A rope
The skin becomes
One of respect
A warrior who bleeds red
And drips in sweat

And
Ladies and Gentlemen
Caesars Palace
Home of champions
Proudly presents
Twelve rounds of boxing
For the Heavyweight
Championship of the World
Six...
Seven...
Eight...
Nine...
You're out

Ding – ding sound the bell
History of the ring
See a-Dempsey's a-spirit
A-hitting
Jack
Jack Manassa

Mauler
See a romance

A-jab-jab
A-jabbing
Send a blow from the soul
Screaming
Dreaming
Contender dream

Jack
A human destruction machine
A fighting hobo
Taking it to him
Or on the retreat
To the sweet canvas
Lying still

Ding-ding sound the bell
History of the ring
See a-Vegas
A-traffic a-rolling
Feel a beat a-missing
Ringside
Here comes a contender
A-bobbing and a-weaving
And screaming
Dreaming contender dream

And somewhere in his gut
Feels a glove a-digging
Roulette wheel spins
On the outside
A contender falls heavily

On the inside
To a disintegrating eye socket
Blood dripping
Mothers crying
Lovers praying
Families dreaming

And from the street
To the ring
It's real fuck it
It's real
It's delicate
It's a dangerous ground to walk

And ding-ding sound the bell
History of the ring
See a-Dempsey's a-spirit
A-hitting
Feel it
Taste it
'Coz someone died tonight
Someone died tonight
Someone died tonight
Fuck it

And
Everlast for all time
Hit me
Punches perfectly thrown
Champions well-groomed
Black boots
Red gloves
Piss blood

WBC
WBA
IBF dreams

Nevada to Atlantic City
There's no escape
A canvas date
Hit me
Work the road
Heavy bag
Skip rope
Dance-dance-dance
Dance to the music
Like a kid from Louisville
Up on his toes talking Olympic gold
So great
Unbeatable
Invincible
Turning invisible

Face on the cover of a magazine
Sensational champion of all time
The brass is high
Then I hear the blues
Of lost souls living low
Nowhere men
And names that forgot
To rise from the mat
Lowered into early graves

'Coz from Hemingway to movie stars
Kings and royalty we're interested
Dear heavyweight champ
Because you're all that's human

And you're all that's true
Sometimes you don't look too good
And you sound a little dumb
But you're fighters not writers

Like there's legal stinks
Money takers and a long
Corrupt count that goes 1 to 14
And just as I stop believing
Something hits me
'Coz God delivers a son
Who shouts out loud

"I refuse to go down
I refuse to lose
I'm unbeatable
I'm invincible
There ain't a man on the planet
That can beat me
My jaw's like concrete
I'm made of iron"

And he skips rope
Dances to the music
Becomes a part of history
The youngest heavyweight champ
With all its emotional vulnerabilities
And all its tragedies
But born on the right day
When all the planets lined up
And gave perfect timing
And Everlast for all time

And born with
WBC
WBA
IBF dreams
That hit you

And
Mirage in the desert
Reflects something going on
Between the lines
Where rich men toast rich men
A toast of nothing

Ice in the glass melts
As fire in the ghetto
Rages into the soul
Of a man reaching out
To a reflection under
Nevada skies
Where his fists will fly
Then floats like Adonis
Out of housing project desire
To a mirage in the sand

On the count of 10
Rich men toast contracts
As a mirror in the desert
Reflects a soul being carried
From a ring and carried home

With eternal crying
Deep – deep inside
And ever – ever so carefully
Dropped back into

Housing project desire

And then the rich men
They toast the rich men
And they laugh out a-loud
In the desert
And
Under African stars
Burning heat
To fight in a jungle
No place of escape
Where warriors roam
Zaire talk
No need for points
In the jungle
The hunter becomes
The hunted
Under African stars

Fighters step through a rope
One fighter
One thinker
Magic in the jungle
Angelo screams
"Get the hell off the rope"

"Don't worry, man
Don't worry, man
Don't worry, man
I'm coming off the rope
To dope
Here I go
Watch me float"

Under African stars
Combinations of new dimensions
Thrown with bad intentions
By a poet
A dreamer
A believer
A speaker man
And slip a right
Off the rope to dope

And under African stars
Where the eclipse of the sun
Is total
A man on a mission
Alone in Zaire
Becomes himself
And becomes a winner
And not no slave name
Like Cassius Clay
But oh yo
Muhammad Ali

And
Sonny days
Lonely grave lying
Under Vegas sand
Sound of jet engines overhead
Hear a rumble
From a restless grave
Sonny on a lonely side
Under cloudy skies
Fighting
Sonny days

Buried a man
Life was a fight
The ring his escape
The grave a place to sleep
I weep
For America and Clay
Sent Sonny away

But always Sonny days
When jets fly overhead
Hear a rumble of a man
In a restless grave
On Sonny days

And
Of Mike Tyson 1990
And HBO was saying
Fire 'n Fear
And we were out
Pounding the streets looking
To disintegrate eye sockets
Switch Channels and
Gene Kelly's Singing in the Rain
Switch back and
It's Fire 'n Fear

We're dancing like middleweights
And striking like heavyweights
And Ladies and Gentlemen
It's the undefeated
Undisputed
One day went east
Down the wrong street
And fell in a heap

You know there was
No more Fire
And no more Fear

And we were out
Searching for
A new network
We were searching
For something different
For something sweet

And Everlast
Stares man in his face
Red gloves
Hang from the door
One statement
Slip me on
Lace me up
Throw a hook
Throw a jab
Let the journalists
Do it in words
Fighters do it with jabs
And let there be
For all times
Hooks
Jabs
And words

For Andy Bernstein
He always beats the count

HINDU IN A JAG

It's kind of funny to see
A Hindu at the wheel of an
Old-dirt-covered-corroding
1970s Jag with an exhaust
Hanging by a thread
He's no untouchable
On a Bombay street
He's LA Jag with a
Totally fucked-up fan belt
And a soot-covered windscreen
And the Jag shakes like
An old Lancaster bomber
One engine down
Return journey
English Channel 1944

Yeah the Hindu sits inside
His dirt-covered-corroding
1970s Jag and smiles
A beautiful smile
Like Peter Sellers
A smile of yeah I know
I'm driving a 1970s
English shit heap
But I'm a Hindu in LA
And there ain't no bloody Empire
Just another puff of smoke
From my dirt-covered-corroding 1970s Jag
It's kind of funny

Z GALLERY

Fade in

At the Z Gallery Print Shop
James Dean jumped out of
The Boulevard of Broken
Dreams print
Stepped out the door
Went across the Burger Ranch
And kind of ordered
A cheeseburger

And at the Z Gallery
The salesman was going
A full revolution looking
For his missing character
And was unable
To finalize a sale

A young stockbroker
Stood before him
With his Amex card
But kept demanding
James Dean be on
The print or no deal

Well Dean walked
All over town!
People pointed
And stared
Saying:
Hey! Haven't I seen
that face before?

Yeah
Yeah
Yeah… I did
The Boulevard of
Broken Dreams print
$49.95 from the Z Gallery
In the steel frame

Well Dean smiled at his
Newfound freedom
And kind of combed his hair
And at the Z Gallery
The salesman was fired
for losing his lead character

Then Dean was stopped
for jaywalking
A cop shouted:
Hey kid!
I don't like your rebel type

Dean kind of turned
And dragged on a cigarette
Then a city slicker arrived
In an open-top Porsche
And said:
Hey, haven't I seen your face
On every stockbrokers wall
From LA to New York?

Clicking his fingers
Yeah
Yeah
Yeah… I did

The Boulevard of
Broken Dreams print
$49.95 from the Z Gallery
In the steel frame

Well then the cop
Realised just who
The rebel character was
Dean panicked
And a fight broke
Dean dragged
The slicker
From the car
Kicked him
And drove off
Heading west

The cop put word out
Over the radio:
The character for $49.95
From the Z Gallery
In the steel frame
Is heading west on Sunset
In a stolen Porsche

Out on the highway
Dean's hair blew in the wind
He felt free
He was out of the Z Gallery
Forever

But in the excitement
He didn't see
An oncoming car

He covered his eyes
And he was back hanging
In the Z Gallery for $49.95

And at the Z Gallery Print Shop
James Dean jumped out of the
Boulevard of Broken Dreams print
Stepped out the door
Went across to the Burger Ranch
And kind of ordered
A cheeseburger

And this went on
And on…
And on…
And on…
And on…
And on…

Fade out

For Nicko Mezzino
The cool one

JERUSALEM

Did you ever step out
Of your door in the morning
Did you ever wish you'd
Stepped out into another City
Other than the one you're in
Or another time?

For me it's back to '76
Back to mad crazy Jerusalem
I'm 17 again
I've got long hair
I'm a free spirit
I feel so untouchable
Like I could walk
Through the Western Wall

Hanging out
Damascus Gate
Like some hip sentry guard
With a loose joint between my lips
Bumping into friends
From this country
From that country
Sitting in Jerusalem
Coffee shops
Jewish youth as optimistic
And crazy as you are

Eating giant chocolate éclairs
They were so big
And cappuccino drinking
We – the – children – free

For our earlier generation
Dreamt it
But they could never have
Imagined it
Through the dark days
Of the 1940s
With the fucking Nazis
Knocking at the door
But this ain't 1940
Or 1945
This is 1976
The disco years

As you hitched a ride
To who knew where?
And crashed by the
Dead Sea
And looked up
At those stars
Stars
Older
Older
Older than Jerusalem
And She is old

Walking from
Tiberia to Magdala
10 shekels in the pocket
But baby it didn't matter
'Coz we could survive
Off the sweat of the land
Of Israel
And you arrived back
At some kibbutz

Muddy and wet
And late for work
But you think
Who cares?
The oranges still got picked
The soccer balls still got kicked
The hash still gave a hit

Walking the Golan
The lights of Syria hung
Like a movie backdrop
In the background
And from there for
One moment in time
Back in 1976
You felt like
You could turn on
The entire world

Israeli F-16s whooshed
Across a hot Negev Desert
So low they'd
Blow-wave your hair
Tilting their wings
To say good morning
As we picked the 6 a.m. melons

And it was back to Jerusalem
Busking guitars in the rain
Two crazy Armenian guys
From the Old City
Dressed like Jake and Elwood
The Blues Brothers

Saying:
Sup the coffee
Smoke the pipe
Crash here for the night
On a bed of stone
A bed of stone

And you do 'coz
You were young
And strong
And getting stronger
All the time
And you were searching
For something Western
And you were searching
For Tel Aviv
And you were desperately
Searching for a neon-flashing
Dance floor
And you knew it wasn't
Studio 54
And you were
Desperately searching
For a bottle of Oxy 10

Yet it was always the same
It was always back
To Jerusalem again
And you were down
By that Wall
Not because you
Were religious
But because you
Were young

And hip
And dead trendy

And as I stood
In my worn-out
Jack Purcell sneakers
Hope in the back pocket
Of my faded 501 Levis
I turned to face the East
I turned to face the West
I turned to face Damascus
I turned to face Amman
I turned to face Cairo
I turned to face the
Dome of the Rock
I turned to face the
Church of the Holy Sepulchre
I turned to face the Mount of Olives
I turned to face the Dead Sea
I turned to face the Red Sea
I turned to face the Rabbis
I turned to face the Priests
I turned to face the Muslims
I turned to face the Druze
I turned to face the Jews
And finally I turned
To face my beloved
Western Wall

And finally
And finally
And finally
I turned to face
The cutest chick

From Memphis Tennessee
And we sat in Jerusalem
Coffee shops eating
Giant chocolate éclairs
They were so big
And cappuccino drinking
We – the – children – free

Well I was young
Back in '76
I was cool
I'm older now
As I stand on
Wilshire Boulevard
And look up at
The Hollywood sign
And I think about
Mt Masada
The land of Israel
Of cappuccinos
Of chocolate éclairs
Of prayer wailing in
From the Old City
From the land of the old
To the land of the new
The brave
Peace and Shalom
All the children of the street

Yeah I was cool
Back in '76
I was young

Today
Well my back aches a little
I need a root canal
The hair's not so long
Not so curly
In fact it's gone
But hey you know
You know
I'm still
Pretty cool

And have you ever
Stepped out of your door in the morning
Did you ever wish
You'd stepped out into another city
Other than the one you're in
Or another time?

Well you know
For me it's back to '76
Back to Jerusalem
All the way back
All the way back
All the way back
All the way back
To mad crazy Jerusalem

For Martin the Chin Weinberg — next year in Jerusalem.

JANICE

Of Janice Joplin
Swirling
Twirling
Tatty hair
Wide flares
Drills its way
Emotionally
Uncontrollably
To the ground
Mascara and saltwater
Covered her face
Man I am drowning

Baby this is a celebration
Senator just a drug inhalation
Mind in confusion
Christ save the children
Just experimentation
Turn to face a nation
A million eyes
Are a-gazing
A child lost in isolation

As swirling
Twirling
Tatty hair
Wide flares
Drills its way
Emotionally
Uncontrollably
To the ground

As the winds blow
Across the decades
It was just a-Janice
Dropping
Dropping
Dropping
Dropping
To her knees
Don't freeze out

JUNK FOOD JUNKIE

KFC
McDonald's
Are working
Dangerously
Junk food's cheap
Helps you sleep
Nervously
3 a.m.
A nightmare
To obscurity
A toilet bowl
Called infinity
Junk Food Junkie
I'll meet you at the cemetery

Doctor open him up
You got a Dunkin' Donut
Stuck in the middle
Of your artery
Cut sharply
I'll identify you
Neurologically
As a Wendy's
Dog meat casualty
I'll prescribe
A world-famous chef
Ask for Wolfgang Puck
The man on Sunset
The world-famous cook

Junk Food Junkie
Junk Food Junkie
Junk Food Junkie

As you drive through
That franchise on the way
To Heaven or Hell
The evil
The evil
The evil
Ronnie McDon
Wishes you well
His Five Star Programmed
Employee of the Month
Who just picked his nose
And touched your pickles
And touched your pickles
And we know he just got over
A dose of the itchy dickle

Junk Food Junkie
Junk Food Junkie
Junk Food Junkie

American experimental mistake
You overweight hopeless case
The next order is
The Pearly Gates
One last fast order
Of over-fried
Uncivilized
Dehumanized
Oil-saturated
Killer fries

Yo!
Yo!
Yo!
Short order cook
Short order cook
Your New York
And LA
Salmonella Burger sucks!

They're Yuck!
I wanna puke up
My guts!
Ashes to ashes
Chicken to burger
It's 100% premeditated
Fucking murder
All you can eat
All you can drink
Suggested soda
Those bubbles
Float upwards
They're guaranteed
To fuck up your motor

It's a two – for – one
Free mass heart attack
Junk Food Junkie
Junk Food Junkie
Junk Food Junkie
God bless you
Junk Food Junkie
Rest in Peace

ONE SECOND IN TIME

1963
So the tale goes
As an Assassin's bullet
Travelled its barrel
Political bullet
Bullet of hate
Psychotic bullet
Intellectual brain
Splatters

Imagine
Nations in tatters
Dreams in shatters
Bullet travels
One second too early
One second too late
My world turns
Alone in space
As America cries
Herself to sleep
So the tale goes

At times dreams
Fall short of reality
Betrayed or let down
As the sun disappears
Behind a dark cloud
But one can only take
A man in his prime when
He stands before you
And cuts it all down
That it's impossible to lie

And says quite simply:

"We do not do it because it is easy
But because it is hard"

And so the tale goes
10
9
8
7
6
5
4
3
2
1
Lift off

As a man touched down
On the moon and beyond
To the brightest star
Where a dream
Becomes a reality
Long
Long
Long
Long after
An Assassin's bullet
Went bang
And so the tale goes

2004
As I stand alone on
The grassy knoll

At 7 a.m. in the morning
With the lights of Dallas
Coming up
I can see so clearly
That November day
40 odd years away

I can see so clearly
John and Jackie waving

I can see so clearly
That motorcade move
Slowly down Houston

I can see so clearly
That slow wide turn
Onto Elm heading to
The underpass
I can see so clearly
The crowds a-cheering

I can hear so clearly
That first shot

I can hear so clearly
That second shot

I can hear so clearly
That third shot

I can hear so clearly
That last fatal shot

I can see so clearly
The chaos in front of me

I can see quite clearly
The book depository

I can see quite clearly
The conspiracy theory
I can see quite clearly
The lone gunman theory

I can see quite clearly
An American Tragedy
And so the tale goes
As I walk away from the
Dealey Plaza I turn
And take one last look
At the grassy knoll
And I can see quite clearly
That optimism
Will never leave me

Today
Today
Yes today
I can see quite clearly

UNBALANCED LOAD

Doing the laundry's
Never no fun
Even on a Sunday
With the dreaded
Loved one
As around
And around
And around it goes
The world is always
Coming home to
An unbalanced load

Blues have gone green
Greens have gone red
Oh, let me back
To fucking bed
Red light indicates
Bleach heads
Carrying Tide
Hung out on
The classifieds
And you wanna throw
Your whole life
Into that wash

All your medications
All your overpriced
Communications
All your debits
All your credits
All your social network
All your neon technical

High-tech Facebook friends
That just have to be
Deleted
In this wash load
I refuse to be
Defeated

All your peace
All your love
All your kisses
All your hugs
All your mystical
Magical crystals
All your secret
Lonely hardcore
One-night stands
All your dirty deeds
Done dirt cheap

And it's like your
Whole life's sitting
On pre-dry
And sometimes
It's a lot easier to laugh
Than it is to fucking cry
As around
And around
And around it goes
We're all just coming home
To an unbalanced load
To a socio-political mess
Yes

Blues have gone green
Greens have gone red
Oh, let me back
To fucking bed
As around
And around
And around it goes
The world is coming home
To a wacky
Wacky
Wacky
Unbalanced
Unbalanced
Unbalanced load

TOMAHAWK

Application for job vacancy
Resume enclosed

Name:
Hawk, Tomahawk, cruise missile

Age:
48

Born:
Waltham, Massachusetts, USA

Experience:
worked under ten presidents
Currently employed

Reasons for seeking new employer:
bored
Looking for a little more action
on the Korean peninsula

Why I'd be right for the position?
I'm never late
Effective infrared nuclear capability
Like to fly;
and arrive unexpected

Most of all
I'm fast
and totally destructive

Made numerous TV appearances on
World News Tonight
NBC Today
CNN with Anderson Cooper
Fox 24-hour news
and an explosive spot on SNL

Taken cameos in numerous motion pictures:
Broken Arrow next to John Travolta,
Crimson Tide with Denzel
and *Patriot Games* alongside Harrison Ford

Favorite foods:
hamburger and fries

Favorite colors:
red, white, and blue

Second favorite country:
Britain

Dislikes:
falafel
dictators
radical Islamic fundamentalists
Places of interest:
Middle East

Like to fly
or take a ship
Either way
I'm pretty fucking quick

I'm happiest
when destroying shit
References:
contact
Donald J. Trump
J.D. Vance,
Marco Rubio

All the best,
Tomahawk

MIDDLE C

Of John Lennon
He found a middle C
And wrote
Another middle C
And a void
With the press
Of a Trigger
He made no music
But a sound
The loudest sound
Ever heard
Not a symphony
But a note
A bad note

Someone's searching
For Van Gogh's ear
Moshe Dayan's eye
Nelson's arm
Art goes on
Even in the rubble
Some men search
Of John Lennon
He found a middle C
And wrote
Another middle C
And a void
Of John Lennon
He found a middle C
And it was good
A good sound
Penny Lane

To Saville Row
To Abbey Road
To 72nd Street on the
Upper West Side
He found a middle C
And wrote

WHITE ROBES

In LA
He wore white robes
Like sheets
He wore white robes
Like sheiks
I don't know if
He was Hindu
Muslim
Or some religious freak
But he wore white robes
To my American ignorance
But on his feet he wore
Nike Air Max in bright red
And that's a fact

RICHARD BURTON

Let's look back in anger
To see a red dragon
With heart beating
Eyes a-glowing
Spirits a-lifted
Life taken in excess

Words that could cut
A prize fighter
Speech sharp as an axe
Blood dripping
Perfect timing
Flawless grooming
A moment in truth
A truth in life

So Shakespeare
Found a protagonist
Like Arthur's sword
Words were safe in hand
And with blood a-dripping
Fire a-raging
King Richard
Took to the stages
From Sloane Square
Kitchen sink
Working around
An ironing board

Intermission

Enter woman
And enter battle
Cutting her down
Like a dry piece of wood
And with books a-flying
Plates a-crashing
Diamonds a-glowing
Cars a-screeching
Scripts a-reading
Hollywood a-waiting
On jet-set path he took
Money at side
Bottle in hand

Words would not return
Running hard
Running fast
Searching for one final act
News spread fast
The red dragon
Had passed

From Geneva
To Chelsea
To Broadway
To the West End
To the Welsh Valleys
King Richard had died

I can still hear the words
Rising from
A Shaftesbury Avenue stage
I can still see the actor
Moving on the silver screen

I can still see
The eyes a - glowing
The fire a - raging
Let's look back in anger
To see the curtain go down
As the lights dim
The theatres empty
Stage door closes

Yet the talk goes on
In the streets
Some things never die
They don't disappear
They don't go gently
Into the night
They are strong
Like gravity
Powerful like the sun
Gentle as the moon
As mad as a crazy poet
On the loose
With pen in hand

Yes I can still see
Richard Burton
Eyes wide
And a-glowing
Fire burning
Words
Words
Words a-flowing
Theatres a-crowding
Projectors a-rolling
Books a-selling

On a life
A life where spirits
Are lifted as high
As life can take you
A spirit lifted high
To the highest of heights

For Sebastian — I'll meet you on the steps of the Royal Court

STAY GREASY BABY

Stay greasy baby
It's a long
Slide down
Yo!
Yo!
Yo!
Don't mean slicking it back
With L'Oreal 'coz I'm worth it
Or slicking it back like
Steven Seagal
Just stay greasy baby
Stay greasy baby
On that long slide down
Yo!
Yo!
Yo!
So you're slipping
And a-sliding down
Down aisle nine
You've got your hands
Deep
Deep
Deep
In the Dippity-Doo
You've got oil
You've got gel
All over you
You're ultimate
You're mega
You're extreme
You're stiff stuff
With total hold

You know what you are?
I'll tell you what you are
You're a slimy-greasy-bastard

And it's Saturday night
It's Saturday night
And you're stuck to your date
You're stuck to your date
She can't break away
She can't break away
She can't break away
She can't twist and shake
She can't twist and shake
You know why?
I'll tell you why
'Coz you're a slimy
Greasy mess
And it's dripping
Out your hair
Down your face
Across your pimples
It's on the ends
Of your chin
It's sticky
Sticky
Sticky
You're a gooey-blob
You're a gooey-blob
You're a gooey-blob
On the disco floor

You're a metaphor
You're like old Pauly Shore

So stay greasy baby
Stay greasy baby
Stay very very greasy
Stay greasy baby
'Coz it's a long slide down

For Chris Slater - Sorry for slamming the door in your face, that's how all good friendships start.

2020 BALL DROP

2020
New York City
Ball Drop
January
February
March
World stops
We're all infectious
Google doctors now

2020 technology
It's got mixed
New
Dazzling
Terminology
Pandemic
Vaccine
Covid19
Lost in isolation
Instagram destination
Mobile workload zoom shows

Wuhan
Biochemical
Bat labs
Snakes
Rats
Designer cats
Cryptic coin
Super stores
Shrink wrapped
Delivered sanitised

For contactless drone
Front door food drops

iPod
Coffee pods
Sex pods
Birth pods
Pods
Pods
Pods

We're all infectious
Google doctors now
Living intellectual bubbles
Keep quarantined
With your doors locked
Or listen to Donny
And drink the Clorox
As he shouted
Look behind ya
It comes from China
Coughing -wheezing
These aren't the symptoms
Of the season

And it was 2020
New York City
Ball Drop
January
February
March
World stops
And we're all infectious
Google doctors now

BROOKLYN-BORN, BROOKLYN-FED

Wild man Jews
Yiddle on the loose
If something's
Not broke
Break it
If you fix it
Break it again
And again

Behind the mic
Anti-comic
Lonely nights
If it's safe
Make it unsafe
'Till it's a dangerous place
Make fun of the blind
'Coz that's a crime

Brooklyn born
Brooklyn fed
Brooklyn in the head.
A one-man institution
A comic revolution
Changing sitcom situations
Wacky character creations

From NBC to HBO
Comedy was on
His marble and rye
In a bubble boy
In a puffy shirt
Sour grapes was a mistake

Seinfeld a fake

Had to escape
To a place called HBO
'Coz on HBO he could say
The word 'fuck'
Make fun of the dead
Survivors
And Tourette's

Through the kvetch
Kvetch
Kvetch
All he ever needed
To say were these three words

Curb Your Enthusiasm

WEST LA GYPSY OF THE 90s

As a perfect stranger
Of the night
Tell me what you think
Of these sunglasses, man

She's Java Coffee Shop
LA froth on top
Dial 1-800-POEM

She's Dior stockings
By day
She's cutaway Levi's
By night

She's stockbroker
325i Hung on
Off-ramps
By day
She's a deadly poet
By night

She's Brentwood Cantor's
American Rag Rodeo
Sprays Giorgio

She's a Century City
Diehard job
She's Democrat
And Republican
She takes lunch
In Westwood
By Monroe's grave

And as a perfect stranger
Of the night
She gets her energy
From neon technicolour
High tech
Chin Chin's Chinese food

She dates
She dates
She dates
An MTV
Corporately manufactured
Designer hippie presenter

She is a West LA
Gypsy of the nineties
And if you stop
And you say hello
I know she's gonna
Blow your mind
And as a perfect stranger
Of the night
Tell me what you think
Of these sunglasses, man

VERSACE

Putting on
This Versace jacket
About to hit the street
I start to think
Of that moment
July 15th 1997
When magic was lost
In a pool of blood
On a Miami floor
Yet no blood
Could ever take away
Style
Colours
Design
Marketing brilliance
A brightness
Pure vision
That hit the runways
Of the world

A party
A mystical
Magical
Fashion show
That went on
And on
And on
Gianni
The Bambino
From Reggio Calabria
Came through Milan
Colours

That dazzle
The mind
Like clothes
Ready to wear
Like priceless works of art

It was a celebrity whirlwind
New York City front row
The champagne flowed
The media growed
GQ
Vogue
And Gianni
Backstage working
Like a mad
Mad
Crazy tailor
A designer watching
A supermodel disappear
Through a door onto a catwalk
Commendatore della Repubblica
Italiana

American Fashion Oscar
For all time
It's in the window
For sale
And sold
So now I hit the streets
I hit the streets
In my jacket
By Gianni Versace

MY TEETH

These teeth
That rot before you
Entered the world
In a better time
When these teeth
Entered the world
Number one on the
British charts was
Dream Lover by
The late Mr. Bobby Darin
Ten years later
Man was walking
On the moon

These teeth
That rot before you
Grew up on
Giant gobstoppers
Sherbert
Or any form of
Rock-hard candy
Available for under
One cent
True nutrition
For teeth that arrived
In a better time
These teeth
Have outlived
Seven dentists
All now dead
Deceased
Gone

Out of here

These teeth
Are a history lesson
On how life can
Become a total fuck-up
For every root
Has been taken
From over forty canals
And every nerve ending
Is now gone
Gone
Gone
Gone
Gone

These teeth
That rot before you
Are now a nice-dark-dull
Colour of life
As no Colgate
No Crest
No Ring of Confidence
Can bring any form
Of commercial whiteness
Back to these pearly whites
They've been
Crowned
Capped
Drilled
And filled
These truly are
The teeth of a poet

These teeth
That rot before you
Saw the last days of
The Beat Generation
Holy Novocaine
Holy pain
Holy cavity
Holy calcium

These teeth
That rot before you
Protested the Vietnam War
High on my grandfather's
Shoulders
Witnessed the assassination
Of JFK
The birth of the Beatles
The invention
Of the colour TV
And www-dot-com

These teeth
That rot before you
Truly are biblical
Industrial
100% Indestructible

For Allen Ginsberg

MEYER

Of Meyer Lanksy
Blood slithered
Down the drain
Washed away
By the rain
Rat-a-tat-a-tat
Meyer Lansky's
On an attack

Administration's
The name of the game
Moving people
Around the town
Without a sound
And cheese slice
Cuts her neck
So precise
Meyer drops a robe
Takes a bath
As he soaks there's
A rat-a-tat-a-tat
On the far side
Of town

A ghost
He walks through
The man in blue
Never pulled no trigger
You boys
You don't have a clue
I'm a businessman
A Jewish immigrant

Is that what's bugging you?

Whether it was
Right or wrong
History was told
Meyer worked in America
He saw
A flag
A flag
A flag of green

And he heard a sound
He heard a sound
He heard a sound
On the far side
Of the town
It went
A-rat-a-tat-a-tat
As the blood slithered
Down the drain
All the evidence
Was washed away
By the rain

With love to Ludlow Street
With love to Katz's Deli
With love to pastrami on rye
With love to Delancey Street
With love to the Lower East Side

SIZZLE SIZZLE

Sizzle-sizzle cheese
Sizzling onion
Sizzling quarter pounder
Saturday night
Greasy burger stand
This is K-L-O-S
Los Angeles
One speaker down
Stereo in mono
Mosquito biting
Burger stand

Here comes
Mr. Wild Horse Records
In a black Trans Am
With a radio scan
But when you go up
You gotta come on down
And on the way down
You gotta meet the people
You fucked on the way up
By the ketchup
And they won't be smiling
They won't be smiling
They won't be smiling
On an L.A. sizzle-sizzle
Drive-in-drive-by
Drop-dead
LA sizzle-sizzle
Griddle
Pickle

WRITTEN ON A MEAD

Come as you are
As you were
As a friend
He wrote it on a Mead
The Mead Corporation
Dayton Ohio
06540 U.S.A

The poet on a Mead
Grunge on a Mead
Seattle on a Mead
A generation on a Mead
Nirvana on a Mead
Love on a Mead
Crazy on a Mead
Magic on a Mead

Kurt wrote history on a Mead
11 inches x 8/2 inches
70 sheets
College ruled
Dayton Ohio
06540 U.S.A.

Kurt Cobain wrote it on a Mead
Come as you are
As a friend

THE TONIGHT SHOW

It's a long
Long road to take
From the open mic to
The Tonight Show
It's like a lightning strike
Comics laying out
The vomit in a Green room
This is his night
In three minutes
He's ready to go
He's throwing one-liners
On the Sunset Strip
Eight-hour valet
Parking shifts
Dollar a Ferrari
Dollar an SUV
Parking them cars
For comedy

Living it big
On a dollar menu
Sitting in the neon
Food franchise
A plastic
Giant
Ronnie McDon
Smiling back

Tranced out on
Another lopsided
LA day that's been
Stolen away

A fused-out Sunset Strip
Ready for another
Ignited night
Of cracked-up
Comedy
Writing
Writing
Writing fast
'Till your brain's crashed

Heading for The Store
To evaluate
And eliminate
All that's not funny
Because it's another
Crazy night lining up
For potluck
Pulling a number from a jar
Get to the mic
Single spot around midnight

Bloodshot eyes transfixed
On an insurance broker
From Minnesota
In town for convention week
He's already boozed up
Half asleep
Trying to get the timing right
Before that red flashing
Reject light craps you out
Like a midnight trainwreck
Ripped off stage
All the comic ghosts crashing
Into the caffeinated comic head

Andy Kaufman – dead
Belushi – dead
Lenny Bruce – dead

'Till one night a voice
Shouts out:

Hey! You're a
Comic revolution
Could become a
One-man institution

Not a Seinfeld
Observation
Not a Dennis Miller
Political assassination
American investigation
You're about to become
An overnight sensation
The original million-dollar
Hollywood Viacom creation

Infrared remotes are
Heading your direction
You're an intoxicating
Media Fix
The new Mr. Ratings
Got perfect timing
You got the mask
Of Jim Carrey
Obscenity of
The Dice
The loony of
Pauly Shore

And now it's time
To walk through
The Tonight Show door

Hit them like
Chris Rock
Give them the magic
Of George Carlin
This is it
Let the last bit
Of vomit flow

Because it's a hazy-insane
Road to go if you
Want to walk out
Onto The Tonight Show

For Richard Lewis
I have your last message in my inbox. Thanks for the advice.

Love to The Comedy Store
Sammy Shore
Mitzi Shore
Pauly Shore
Thank you

THE CAT

Cat Stevens was playing
In the background
And the man behind
The coffee bar in L.A.
Had a great idea
For a screenplay
The scientific building
Of the Panama Canal
Not only did they build
A great canal but found
A cure for malaria

I said: "Write it"

He said he was too busy
Working on the theory of
Three-dimensional chess
But we both agreed
The canal idea would
Probably bring in an
Academy Award for Best Picture
All this took place on a Monday
There were still 40 cups to go
'Till Friday

And The Cat
Well The Cat
The Cat
The Cat
The Cat
Just kept on playing

SWEET AND LOW

We're complicated
Complex cosmopolitans
On the brink of oblivion
As she pours another
Sweet 'n Low

Don't know what it is
About a woman
That makes you
Shiver and shake
And always seems
To send you
Back to bed

I think I know what
Your problem is
You've been out
On too many late dates
It's the smell of wild scent
The taste of Chardonnay
And rock 'n roll all night
Like that song by Prince
You know the one - Kiss
Kiss
Kiss
Kiss
Always seems to start
The same way
One little kiss
That rearranges the poetry
That sends you hazy
A little obsessively crazy

As Around
And around
And around
And around
The town you go
Eating out at all the right places

Around
And around
And around
And around
The town you go
Sucking on each other's juices
Watching reruns of I Love Lucy
Video classics
Bottles of red
And packets of condoms
From that place in the '80s
You know the place Condomania

Yeah!
We're complicated
Complex cosmopolitans
On the brink of oblivion
As she pours another
Sweet 'n Low
Against the backdrop
Of a late-night W Hotel
But this relationship
Was deep
It was supposed to last
It was a relationship
That had already reached
A 26-CD collection

Well she split last night
And well she split the discs
And well I'm left with six
But hey! - I kept
The Best of
Mr. Barry Manilow

Still, what more
Can one ask for
From a relationship
That started with
The spotting of a
Pair of sexy legs
In the produce section
Of the supermarket?

Still, what more
Can one ask for
From a long-legged
Complex-relationship
That devours you
That devours you
That devours you
That devours you whole
Yeah!
We're complicated
Complex cosmopolitans
On the brink of oblivion
As she pours another
Sweet 'n Low against
The backdrop of a
Late-night W Hotel

For Holly Dolly — "Roll em"

WILDE

Wild about
Oscar Wilde
Round the Vile Bodies Club

Wild about Oxford
On a summer's day

Wild about Ernest
The importance of

Wild about
Lady Windermere's Fan
In black and white on the BBC

Wild about
Cucumber sandwiches
And comedy coming at me

Yes, I'm wild about
Humour
Wild about
Words
Wild about
Art

Yes, I'm wild about Wilde

KANISH

Standing on the corner
Of 46th and 6th
Here in the big red
Moving neon balls
Comes the news
From Fox and
The Associated Press
Whoever they are
Because tell me
Does God make
The news for the media
Or does the media
Make the news for God
Or do they just sit
High above the Rockefeller
And kinda cut a deal?

And as I stand minute
On the corner
An Iranian hotdog man
Stands a long way
From Tehran
Nowhere near
The Koran
Selling cold-shitty
Kinish
Oh Kanish!
Kanish!
Kanish!
To a Manhattan
Corporate man

And as my world
Turns in space
The news comes
Around again
And again
Violent crime's
Down 9.2%
And the army's
Top enlisted man says

"Hey I never dropped my pants
Nor did the President"

This is Thursday
The 2nd of October
Nineteen hundred and ninety-seven
A.D
Partly cloudy
Chance of scattered rain
Oh Kanish!
Kanish!
Kanish!

As the news comes
Around again
And again
And again
A plane's down
In the Himalayas
245 dead in the mist
Not far from Tibet
Where Richard Gere
Hangs out

Pulling gerbils
Out of his ass

Which is not far from
Everest
Which is not far from
Outer space
Where astronauts
And cosmonauts
Waltz around in a
Scientific tin can
With their one billion dollar
Infrared nuclear
Laser repair kits

And for one second
I know they can see
All the way down
To 46th and 6th
And with their satellite dish
I know they can see
The Kanish!
Kanish!
Kanish!

And as the wind blows
Up The Avenue
Of the Americas
The Dow is daytime trading
Tech stocks holding steady
As the rich get richer
The poor get more envious
And the Kanish!
Well, the Kanish!

The Kanish!
Gets a little colder
As the news comes
Around again
And again
And again

But right now
Ya! know
Ya! know
I think I will go
Have myself
A cold-shitty
Kanish!

Oh, Kanish!
Kanish!
Kanish!

LOS ANGELES

Fade in

Los Angeles
Take one
Action

Words
Perfectly-selected
Coffee bars
Well-picked
Waxed legs
Faxed face
I spell well
Shakespeare
Wrote for I

Shades of light from
A one-touch phone
Splash in a pool
Don't get wet
You're just an iced-tease
You got a mono-disease
Well, ain't we a city slicker?
I'll have an ice-whipped
Coffee mocha please
And you're a ghost
You walk through parties
Unseen
Unheard
Untouched
And graduated
And you're a

Magazine's dream
Like a coloured page
In Cosmo
Like a page in GQ
You're Porsche
Ferrari
You can push a divorce
And you're big news
On the screen
Los Angeles
Take two
Action

Desires on Get Rich
Desires on Rodeo
Desires on Limo
Desires on Rich Eyes
Desires on Him
Desires on Her
Desires on LA

Cut

PSYCHO VINNY

It's Saturday night
Lights down
Fade in
A magic movie evening
But oh no
Psycho Vinny's one seat
Behind you
A-yapping
And a-yapping
And a-yapping
And he won't
Shut the fuck up

He's going on
And on
And on
And he's right behind you
He's got that L'Oreal gel
Smelling of Brute
A cheap polyester suit
And he's going on
And on
And on
A-yapping
And a-yapping

He's drawing on his
Sweet popcorn
Conclusions
He's got Academy Award
Illusions
He's Al Pacino

He's Al Pacino
He's Al Pacino
In his wildest of dreams
And he's going on
And on
And on
A-yapping
And a-yapping

He's about as interesting
As a Woody Allen
Analysation
On the art of
Masturbation
And he's going on
And on
And on
He's drawing on his
Sweet popcorn
Conclusions
He's got Academy Award
Illusions

The usher shines a torch
Into Vinny's blotchy mush
He's up in platform shoes no less
He's got that John Travolta
Saturday Night Fever strut
He's got a mad-mad-glazed
Robert De Niro look
He shouts out like Joe Pesci
"I'll pop your fucking eyes"

I've had a fucking nuff
I get up

Vinny flicks his ticket stub
Into my 7Up
I hit the floor
Like Rocky Balboa
The New York law
Show Vinny the door

Lights down
Fade in
The audience is
A-listening
But oh no
Psycho Vinny
Is one seat behind you
A-yapping
And a-yapping
And he won't
Shut the fuck up
You can hear Vinny
Slurping
Slurping up his 7Up
Lights down
Fade in
Yeah! It's Saturday night
That magic movie evening
But oh no
Psycho Vinny's one seat
Behind you
A-yapping
And a-yapping
And he won't
Shut the fuck up
Just that slurping
On his 7Up

UNDERWOOD

Sometimes I want to switch
From my Apple Mac PowerBook
Onto a 1950s Underwood
And bang out the words hard
Tap – tap – tap
And there's the bell
As you recoil

Tap – tap – working hard
Thoughts of life
On an old Underwood
Smoke fills the air
My pack of Lucky Strikes
Sit next to a cold beer
And there's the bell
As you recoil

I'm drifting back in time
Censorship is everywhere
You've got to dance
Between the words
Between the lines
One sentence
One publisher
And you are that close
To a trial on morality
On political correctness
One word from being banned
One sentence that leads to jail
But this is 2025
As I sit on my antiseptic
Mac PowerBook

I can say
Fuck you arsehole
And the spellcheck
Underlines it

Somehow I like the sounds
Of a 1950s Underwood
Just less understood
Feels more Hollywood
Feels more East Village
Feels more a time
When you're writing
And some agent is
Just outside the door
Some Judge
Some Cop
Some Authority
Is going to bust in
As you tap – tap – tap
On your 1950s Underwood

SUBURBIA

Suburbia
A crazy
Whacked-out
Human ideology
Modern mythology
Next door to a
Designer shed
Breaking Bad
Meth lab
Teeth-bearing
Slightly damaged pit-bull
On command to attack
Any shadow that moves
Just left of the flyscreen

Next door to
Part-time porn stashers
Full-time street taggers
On chronic synthetic
Sending out false
Smoke ring tweets
To Big Bang Theory
White extremist geeks
Homemade game-changers
Channel 7 Breaking News
Detonators
Lonely keyboard
Gladiators

A legless Digger
Who pinned his future
On an idea

He could make peace
with the Taliban
In Afghanistan
But peace don't sell
Down in the burbs
Suburbia ain't paying
A streaming bill for peace
No

What they really want to see
Is a Tomahawk cruise missile
Hit a fucking falafel stand
Like sands through
A deranged hourglass
So are the twisted
Days of our lives

Let's get ready for
One-minute
Seismic brain snaps
Downloaded generic
Pop charts
A script on tap
For tapped-up Prozac
On a Kurt Cobain
Suicide soundtrack

A 4.9% APR finance
Or $1,000 cashback
On any dreamed-up
Sales pitch
That hits the left side
Of the north side
Of the brain

That's become chemically
Unbalanced
Courtesy of Coles
Neon-technical-tomatoes
Scientifically reformed
Food molecules
That are just
Oversized
Overgrown
Sex-reducer hormones
That turn an
Insurance salesman
Into a blood-deranged
Mass murderer on a vigilante
Neighbourhood Watch-scheme
To protect the guilty

Money Street
Lost in the GPS
Of Australia
And normal is
Any suburban door
You knock on
Turn the lock on
Walk in on
We can fit ya
Lift ya
Save ya
And slip ya
Into a perfect
Aussie cubic system
In a place called
Suburbia

LA SOAP

How I'd love to be
A Los Angeles
Soap Opera Star
I'm Young
I'm Restless
I'm Bold
I'm Beautiful
I've seen
The Guiding Light
But I only have
One Life to Live

Yet I never drove
A Ferrari to the studio
Seduced Susan Lucci
Then between Mintoes
And Tasters Choice
Became a low down
Dirty Scoundrel
And plot to kill
Her millionaire
Diabetic husband
While I secretly
Replace his insulin
With a deadly poison
And dump the body
In a Hollywood jacuzzi
As I slowly pump away
On Susan Lucci
Then she shouts out
"Stop
 Stop

Cos it's not you I want
All I really want
Is a daytime Emmy
A daytime Emmy
And my face on the cover
Of TV Guide!"

Cut to commercials

And as I walk
Supermarket reality
There on the cover of
Soap News Weekly
Is a picture of Lucci
With a hairy-hairy-hairy
Two-headed baby
And I realise Soaps
Are totally fucking crazy
And as she sits
Alone in the dark
At Cedars Sinai
The young doctor arrives
She gives him the eye
"Your husband's touch and go
On a drip I'm sorry
We'll know in a couple"
He leaves
She sits alone and thinks
'Christ the prick's still alive'
Thoughts of
Creeping in the room
Pulling his drip
Sending him to sleep
A quick trip

To the Wells Fargo
A fuck in a limo
She crosses her legs
She sprays a little Giorgio
And waits for Lieutenant Colombo

And how I'd love to be
A Los Angeles
Soap Opera Star
I'm Young
I'm Restless
I'm Bold
I'm Beautiful
I've seen
The Guiding Light
But I only have
One Life to Live

HENRY MOORE'S AT THE DOOR

Art is corporate
And corporates art
Knock - Knock
Henry Moore's at the door
Warhol's Brillo
Peter Mack in a flash
Pow-crash-smash
All comes trashing together
Like a cucumber sandwich
Contemporary colourful rainfall
Opening on Rodeo

Art is corporate
And corporates art
Sold to Sylvester Stallone
Sold to Ralph Lauren
Wrap it up
And get it out the door
Just past the Henry Moore

THE FROSTY FLAKE SURFER

Last night I thought to myself
Life sure is tough on the
Minimum wage
I looked at my girl in bed
Reading her Hello magazine
And she looked uninterested
I was uninterested
Thought to myself
Sure is funny
Man spends half his life
Dreaming about what
He wants to be
And the other half
Why he never became it

Then I remembered
I slipped
I slipped
I slipped
I slipped into a dream
I dreamt I fell through
The hole of my Cheerios
Into a bowl of milk
And I sank
And it was awful

Then I remembered
I had another dream
I dreamt I fell into
The bowl of milk
But I didn't sink

No - I landed on
A frosty flake

Well, first I was floating
On the flake
Then I was surfing
On the flake

You know what I was?
I was a cool
Frosty Flake Surfer
That morning
I crept out of bed
Leaving her snoring
I went down the store
And bought five boxes
Of these Frosty Flakes
I came home and threw
The Cheerios in the trash

That morning I was
Crunching away over
Breakfast and she
Looked up over the top
Of her Hello magazine
At Mr. Minimum Wage
But I knew
I knew I was the
Cool
Cool
Frosty Flake Surfer
And there wasn't a
Fucking thing she could
Do about it

HOBO JOE

Tonight I'm
I'm on the town
But right now
I'm in the store
As I walk the aisle
On my own I spot
The Hobo Joe shampoo
It only costs ten bucks
But they say it's the best

And the conditioner's on sale
Only eight bucks
Your hair will
Gleam and shine
And you'll feel fine
And the promotions girl says
I can have you smelling fine

So she sprays me
With her Aramis
And she sprays me
With her Dior
And well I spray her
With twenty-five bucks

And don't forget
Your dental floss
And your underarm
And your vitamin E
It's good for your hands
And it's good for your face
Well, now it's dark

As I approach the bar
My hair's shining
My teeth are gleaming
And like the Aramis
Is stinking
And then the bouncer
Gives me one weird look

And says: "Sorry guy, no jeans"
I said, "No jeans?"
He said, "No jeans"
I said, "No jeans"
He said, "No jeans"

And then you walk
The streets alone
And sit down
Next to an old tramp
Who sniffs you up and down
And he shouts out
Oh no, not Aramis
And then he gets up
And walks away
Into the distance
Leaving you alone
In the gutter
Gleaming
And shining
And stinking
Of Aramis

And tonight
I'm on the town
But right now
I'm in the store

KEROUAC

Walking through City Lights
The mist coming off the bay
I feel a-spirit rise to the top
Of Piedmont-Oakland Hills
Downing a drink in Vesuvius
And crossing Chinatown
I think of Jack's words

And as I cross
The Golden Gate
I think of those lines
That he put down
In a rush of truth
I think that the earth
Was never dark
Never dull
When Jack strolled it's gravel
Coming to us from Lowell
Massachusetts
Kerouac the outsider
Kerouac the rebel
Kerouac on
The Steve Allen Show
Kerouac the entertainer
Kerouac on the road
Kerouac in our souls
Words spoken in jazz
Jazz!
Jazz!
Jazz!
Steamy smoke-filled bars
From MacDougal Street

Washington Square Park
To Washington Heights
To the south
To the horizons
Of our minds
Spirits rising
In prose
In poetry
In flight
In fight
No room for the phoney
Pseudo-intellectuals
Just room for inspiration
Of shining light

And now you rest in the earth
Back home in Lowell
I'll never forget that day
I stood there alone
Just me and Jack
And I felt the words
Rising!
Rising!
Rising up!
And as I walked away
I had to stop and look back
And just say: "Thanks Jack"

And I never came back
I just started moving
The pen across the napkin
In the coffee bars
Day after day

From New York
To LA

And living my life
The only way I could
OUT LOUD

VICTORIA'S SECRET

She enters the bedroom
To fix her Sunday face
Mr. America's alone
Off a nine – to – five week
She's left her supplement
Under the classifieds
Oh, Victoria's Secret
One's own secret
Victoria what's your secret
Of lace and negligee?
Pages smell
Of a scent giveaway
He leaps onto the page
Her perfect breasts
Flash in his face

"What's your name?" Victoria asks

"Mr. America
From suburbia" he says

"Oh, Mr. America
From suburbia
Will you do me a favour?"

"Yes, Victoria
Anything
Anything
I'll empty your trash
Your waste disposal
Anything
Anything"

"Yes, Mr. America
But first do me a favour"

"Yes – anything – anything"

"Mr. America
Make love to me
Take off my Victoria bra
My Victoria stockings
My Victoria panties
Oh, fuck me
Fuck me
Fuck me hard"

"Oh yes, Victoria"
"Oh yes, Mr. America"
"Oh yes, Victoria"
"Oh yes, Mr. America"

"Oh, Victoria let's go
Onto page two together
Maybe the whole supplement"

"No, Mr. America
From suburbia
I hear your wife
She's out the bathroom
Kiss me one last time"
They kiss
Mr. America
Jumps off the page
His wife returns
From the bathroom
Screeching

Screeching
Screeching

"Where's my supplement?
Where's my supplement?"

She snatches the supplement
And returns to the bathroom
With Victoria
But Mr. America knows
Victoria's secret
He knows the secret
He knows
Victoria's Secret

SACRED GROUND

Grinding
Winding
Woke to the sounds
Of dump truck music
Paracetamol head
Grinding
Winding out that
Manchester laneway

There's not much left
Across that laneway
Just skin and bones
Of some scrumptious duck
Turned to muck
Thrown into the
Manchester dump truck

Total madness awaits me
The grinding sends me
Nervous system
Fucking crazy
The bathroom delays me
First piss I miss
And hit me feet
I feel dead beat
At the toilet seat
Not like the Holy Trinity of
Best – Law – and – Charlton

Press down the finger
On the can
In the sink

There's a giant mountain
Of Gillette foam

I'm inspired
Tonight I think
I'll turn on the TV
And watch United
If we win we'll all be
Bleeding excited

I cut the shave
There's a drop of blood
But I feel good
There's no sound
That grinding's gone away
To attack another neighbour
And I realize now
I'm in Manchester
And I realize I must be
Walking on
Walking on
Walking on
Sacred ground

For George Best
For Bobby Charlton
For Denis Law
For Sir Matt Busby
February 6th 1958
For The Flowers of Manchester
The sun always rises over the Stretford End

CHECK

Check
Check One
Check Two
Check Three
Knock three times
And don't fucking come in
I'm a poet
A prophet
A star
And hey, you
Go look at me
100-foot-long car
And don't touch
Me fucking guitar

'Ave have you got
Your bleeding
Backstage pass?
'Coz you sound
A little daft to me
And you're nobody
'Till you're like me
A paranoid rock-n-roll
Schizophrenic
Suicide potential
Fucking the devil
On the front of the Enquirer
I'll give 'em news
I'll give 'em news
I'll give 'em news
I'll piss
I'll piss

I'll piss on
The Interactive
House of Blues

I've been to the Carly Simon
How to Survive the Paparazzi
On Martha's fucking vineyard

Check One
I'm available on disc
Check Two
I'm available on laser
Check Three
I'm available on
Interplanetary satellite system

Check One
Check Two
Check Three
Knock three times
And don't fucking come in
I'm a poet
A prophet
A star
And hey – you!
Go look at me
100-foot-long car
And hey, don't touch
Me fucking guitar
And hey – you!
'Ave you got your
Bleeding backstage pass?

Check One
Check Two
Check Three
Knock three times
And don't fucking come in
I'm a poet
A prophet
A Manchester starrrr

For John Robb, for Tony Wilson. Thank you.

INDIE MAN

Everybody wants
To be a star
Everybody wants
To go far
Everybody's looking
For that supernova in the sky
I've got the words
He's got the birds
Yeah! Everybody wants
To be a star
Everybody wants
To go far
Everybody wants
To sell that indie merch
Get on the indie bus
Get on the indie tour
Be in that indie band
Get behind that indie mic
Go to the indie bank
Yeah! Everybody wants
To be a star
Everybody wants
To go far
Everybody's heading
Up to Manchester

For Alan McGee, we will always be in the booth looking out on sunset.

THE FINAL BEAT

Words of poets flow
Spilling verse
On napkins
Words written
From MacDougal Street
To North Beach
Coffee stained
Words percolating
Through caffeinated veins

Political verse
Geographical verse
Comical verse
Change of verse
Freedom of verse

Folk verse
Punk verse
Rock verse
Rap verse

From mind
To napkin
Hours passed
Ink flowed

For the poets
In conversation
Interaction

In the beats
Streets
Written
By freaks
And geeks
Lawyer poets
Dentist poets
Surgeon poets
Wall Street poets
Cab driver poets
Convict poets
Slam poets
2026
AI poets
Dead poets

We must be careful
Before we're silenced

BELOWSKOLOGY

I was hanging
On the King's Road
World's End
Conrad Hotel
Lots Road
Harbour Yard
Moving between
Obscurity
And celebrity

Driving Porsches
Flying First Class
Then back on
The number 11 bus
Picking up a box
Of dead man's clothes
At the Chelsea Hospital
He was Ian Fleming's butler
I'm told

Riding round Sloane Street
With royalty in the next seat
16th in line to the throne
As I hit the brakes
In a way this is
Belowskology

I'm reciting poetry
To Lisa Marie Presley
Then sitting outside
The Laurel Canyon
Country Store

Love Street
As John Denver
Walked out the door

Doing spoken word shows
At the Hollywood Standard Hotel
Sitting caged
In a holding cell at JFK
Delivering a million dollars' worth
Of Bulgari jewels
To the Mallorca Hills

Taxi driver says
"Ah, Señor
You want Miss Schiffer?"

Claudia says
"You want to crash the night?"

I say
"Nah I wanna head to Shagaluf."

Then again
It was back to
New York City
Tea with Allen Ginsberg

I was asked to write a book
How all these things add up
I lose track of time
They drift through my mind
Decades lost
In time and rhyme
Like distant dreams

Cinematic flashes

Yeah! I remember
In the bank
0.7 cents
Wow I'm still in credit
See - a million dollars
Have passed through this account
But I cannot tell you about that
I can say this
"Guess I missed the bank
And underestimated
What I need"

A friend once sang
Those words to me
On a rainy night
In Manchester

Then again as you read
The poems in this book
I am sure the balance
Has gone up
You may see me
You may not
P.S. Just having a chat
To the U.S. Ambassador
To Australia
Then lunch with
The mayor of the city
Then meeting up with
A shady character
Called Vince

It's just a day in the life of
Belowskology
Hope you enjoyed this collection
As I run with words
That are all jumbled up
And hey! - Don't forget
To buy the merch
Love Belowsky... x

EDITORIAL AFTERWORD

It is significant for the poems of Stephen Belowsky to be collected in print after so much of his career has existed on stage. In publishing this collection it places them under a different kind of spotlight. Not the one in which Belowsky has carved his niche, but the judgment of the reader: leafing through the pages of a paperback stripped from his unique charisma. It's noteworthy too that his verses occupy the notion of the printed page. In *Z Gallery* we follow the image of James Dean breaking free from a framed poster housed in a gallery to wreak havoc. In *Victoria's Secret,* a married man jumps into an affair with the pages of a newspaper supplement.

Belowsky's subjects include Kerouac, coffee and suburbia.
The truth about his work? It should be cliché.
Yet somehow he manages to evade this.

How? It's worth quoting the late Californian sculptor Ken Price, whose illustration is printed on the cover of this volume and joined by Belowsky, occupies the realm of funk quite comfortably...

"You don't have to act serious to be serious."

...Honk

020-DESK-ZERO